The Second Green Goblin Book

Have you ever heard of a shop which offers to get *anything* for *anyone*? There's one in this book, run by three goblin friends, Tuppeny, Feefo and Jinks. Little Tuppeny is round as a ball and can be frightened easily – but he's a jolly little fellow who keeps the others cheerful. Feefo can make the most extraordinary noises – anything from a train to two dragons having a fight – and that comes in useful sometimes. And wily Jinks, the goblin pedlar, usually has *something* useful in his tray of goods that can help them out of a fix – to say nothing of his pet white mouse who can sometimes be the most use of all.

THE SECOND GREEN GOBLIN BOOK

by

Enid Blyton

Illustrated by
Paul Crompton

RED FOX

A Red Fox Book
Published by Random House Children's Books
20 Vauxhall Bridge Road, London SW1V 2SA

A division of Random House UK Ltd.
London Melbourne Sydney Auckland
Johannesburg and agencies throughout the world

First published as The Green Goblin Book by Newnes 1935
Shortened version (Feefo, Tuppeny and Jinks) published by Staples
Press 1951

Red Fox edition 1993

Set in Plantin
Phototypeset by Intype, London

Printed and bound in Great Britain by
Cox & Wyman Ltd, Reading, Berkshire

ISBN 0 09 993710 7

Contents

The Strange Land of Topsy-Turvy

One morning, when Tuppeny, Feefo and Jinks, the three Goblins who ran a shop offering to get *anything* for *anyone*, were scrubbing their floor, they heard a great sound of cheering and hurrahing outside. They dropped their brushes and dusters to see what it was and rushed outside.

'Jumping beetles! It's the King and Queen of Fairyland!' cried Tuppeny, in excitement. 'Ooh! They're driving through Heyho Village! Let's go and cheer them!'

Just as they got to their gate the shining golden carriage of the King and Queen drove up. The goblins, thinking that the carriage was going past, waved their hands and cheered loudly. Tuppeny's voice was so enormous that it almost deafened everyone.

And then – and then – to the three goblins' great astonishment, the golden carriage

7

stopped at their very gate, and the King and Queen got out!

The goblins stood and stared with wide eyes and open mouths. Were their Majesties coming to visit *them*? Oh, no, surely not!

But, you know, they were! Yes, they walked right up to the gate, smiling, their jewelled crowns winking and blinking in the sun, and their long and beautiful wings gleaming like the wings of summer dragon-flies!

'Is this the shop belonging to Tuppeny, Feefo and Jinks?' asked the King.

'Yes – yes, certainly it is! Oh, yes, Your Majesty!' stammered Jinks, so much surprised that he didn't even move away from the gate.

Feefo, always the polite one, pulled him away and hissed into his ear. 'Can't you bow, you great stupid? Can't you even move out of the way?'

Jinks at once bowed deeply and made way for their Majesties. The King and Queen walked up the garden and into the little shop. Feefo got chairs, dusted them and put a pail of dirty water out of the way. Tuppeny was so overcome with awe and surprise that he didn't do or say anything at all. He just stood and stared.

'This is a great honour,' said Feefo to the King and Queen. 'Is there anything we can do for Your Majesties?'

'We have heard of you and the wonderful things you have done,' said the Queen, in a high, silvery voice like a swallow's. 'And as we are in a difficulty ourselves, we wondered if perhaps you could help us, as you have helped others.'

'Oh, Your Majesty, we'd love to!' said Jinks, standing first on one leg and then on the other,

9

in the greatest delight. He could hardly keep from stroking the Queen's fine silky hair, that shone like golden sunlight. What a day this was! What an honour!

'This is our difficulty,' said the King. 'In Topsy-Turvy Land there lives an Enchanter, called Know-All, and he's just like his name. In fact, he knows too much, and his magic and enchantments are getting far too powerful for our happiness. He can spirit away fairies and elves, and we don't know where they've gone to. So we wondered if you could go to Topsy-Turvy Land and capture him for us.'

'Jumping beetles!' said Tuppeny, in the greatest alarm. He didn't at all like the idea of capturing a powerful enchanter. Feefo looked a little startled, but Jinks, as usual, was only too pleased to have a job to do. He beamed all over his jolly face at once.

'Yes, Your Majesty, we'll see to that at once for you. You can trust us! We'll do our very best.'

'For reward we will give you a palace on a hill, with a most marvellous view,' said the Queen. The goblins looked at one another. A palace! My, wouldn't they be grand! They would be like princes!

'Well, that's settled then,' said the King,

rising. 'Thank you very much. Let us know when you have captured the Enchanter and we will deal with him.'

Their Majesties went back to their golden carriage, waved goodbye and drove off, their eight white horses galloping fast down the village street. As soon as they were gone, their friend, the fairy Tiptoe, came rushing in to hear what the visit had been about.

But when she heard what they had to do, she grew pale and shook her head.

'You'll never capture Know-All,' she said.

11

'He is one of the most powerful and wicked enchanters in the whole world. He is worse than a bad witch. You are clever, Jinks darling, but not so clever as Know-All.'

'D-d-d-d-don't let's g-g-g-go!' stammered Tuppeny, in a fright.

But Jinks only grinned. He had a great belief in himself, and besides, hadn't he promised the King and Queen to try? He couldn't break his word.

They took out their maps and looked up Topsy-Turvy Land. It was rather a long way away. First they had to go through Pixie-Land, then over the Land of Night and last of all through the Grumbling Wood. Ooh dear!

Tuppeny didn't like the sound of things at all.

'Well, Tuppeny, you can stay at home, if you like, and mind the shop,' said Jinks. But Tuppeny wouldn't hear of that. Yes, he was afraid, but he wasn't a coward. He was coming too!

'I'll mind the shop for you,' said Tiptoe. 'But, oh, I do hope you won't be too long, goblins, because I shall be dreadfully worried about you.'

The next day they set off for Pixie-Land. They drove away in their little green motor-car and Tiptoe waved to them from the gate. By the afternoon they had come to Pixie-Land. It was a pretty place, full of houses built of big toadstools, painted all kinds of bright colours. The pixies were little chattering folk, and the goblins waved cheerfully to them as they went by.

They had tea in Pixie-Land at a Toadstool tea-house, and a very good tea it was, especially some little pink cakes made of ripe wild strawberries and moonlight sugar. Tuppeny ate so many that he fell asleep in the car afterwards and didn't wake up until they were in the Land of Night. This was a strange land, always dark, even in the daytime, with great silver stars in the sky and a moon that looked three times as big as it ought to be. Only night-time creatures lived there – big, silent-winged owls that hooted frighteningly in Jinks's ear, black bats that squeaked piercingly as they flew over the car, and strange, shadowy creatures that fled out of the way of the headlights.

'I only hope our car doesn't break down here,' said Jinks, a little bit scared.

'Jumping beetles!' said Tuppeny, in a fright. 'Do you think it will?'

But it didn't. It chugged on well and at last

the sun rose on the Grumbling Wood, which stood next to the Land of Night.

The Grumbling Wood was a very difficult place to drive in. Big tree-roots suddenly stood up in the car's way and bushes seemed to appear out of nothing. The trees were tall and dark, and their leaves were queer. They were silver on the upper surface and black underneath, and when the wind blew the whole forest shimmered and shone in the strangest way.

And it grumbled! The trees groaned and grunted. The bushes sighed as if their hearts

14

were breaking. Even the flowers hung their heads down and made a curious whining noise that could just be heard. It was a most unhappy place.

'These wretched tree-roots that keep popping up and nearly upsetting us!' grumbled Feefo – but Jinks nudged him sharply on the arm and spoke to him in a low whisper.

'Now, Feefo, don't grumble, whatever you do! Those who grumble belong to the wood and we don't want to stay here for the rest of our lives! You just watch, and you'll see some folk who have grumbled and groaned when they went through here and have had to stay for always!'

Feefo and Tuppeny looked out – and sure enough, here and there in the wood were some odd, unhappy-looking folk, with long faces. Some were scolding each other. Some were walking along, grumbling to themselves. Some were sighing at the heavy bundles they carried.

'My goodness, I shan't say a single grumble again!' said Feefo, startled. 'I shouldn't like to live with these grumblers in this strange, Grumbling Wood!'

At last, almost jolted to bits by the jutting tree-roots, the unexpected bushes and the low-hanging branches, the goblins left the

Grumbling Wood behind, and came to Topsy-Turvy Land. And here they really had to stop the car and gaze in astonishment.

For everything was topsy-turvy! Even the houses were built upside down. The people walked on their hands as Jinks sometimes did, and wore hats on their feet. The dogs had cats' tails, and the cats barked like dogs. Horses wore horns and the cows had coats like sheep. Really, the goblins could hardly believe their eyes!

Then they saw a large notice standing by the roadside. The notice was upside down, of course, but Jinks, by standing on his hands,

16

could easily read it. He came back to the others in excitement.

'I say, it's a notice from Know-All, the Enchanter. He says he is willing to give anyone a magic wand if they can do three things.'

'What are they?' asked Tuppeny and Feefo.

'One is – to show him something that nobody has ever seen before,' said Jinks. 'The second is to dance on the rock outside his palace and kick dust from it – and the third is to tell him what he is thinking!'

'Quite impossible, all three of them!' groaned Feefo. 'What's the use of bothering about a notice like that, Jinks?'

'What's the use!' cried Jinks. 'I'll tell you, Feefo! I can do all those things!'

Tuppeny and Feefo stared at him as if he had gone mad.

'Do you feel all right?' asked Tuppeny, anxiously. 'You're sure you don't feel ill, Jinks?'

'Don't be silly,' said Jinks, his bright eyes shining. 'My wits are as sharp as the Enchanter's, though I don't know nearly as much magic as he does! I tell you, I can do all these things!'

'You're a clever fellow, Jinks,' said Feefo. 'Well, tell us what you're going to do.'

But Jinks wouldn't. He said it was to be a

secret. He loved secrets and he loved surprising people. He jumped into the car again with the others and drove off through Topsy-Turvy Land. He stopped when he met a postman, walking on his hands, of course, and asked him where the sweep lived.

'That's his house over there,' said the postman, pointing. Jinks drove over to it and was surprised to find a little notice there that said –

> MISTER BISCUIT, THE SWEEP.
> ALL WASHING
> DONE HERE.

Mister Biscuit stood at his door, upside-down. 'Are you the sweep?' asked Jinks.

'Yes,' said Mister Biscuit.

'Have you any soot for sale?' said Jinks.

'Bless us, no!' said Mister Biscuit. 'I may be the sweep, but I don't sweep chimneys. I wash clothes.'

'What a funny idea!' said Feefo. 'I should hate to live in this land where everybody does the work that somebody else should do!'

'Who sweeps the chimneys, then?' asked Jinks, impatiently.

'Mister Chop, the washerman,' said Mister

Biscuit, getting out his handkerchief and blowing his ear with it. Tuppeny giggled and Mister Biscuit frowned at him.

'Where does he live?' asked Jinks.

'He lives at the fishmonger's,' said Mister Biscuit, and went indoors, angry with Tuppeny because he wouldn't stop laughing.

So Jinks drove to the fishmonger's, but as he sold cakes and bread, it was a very curious fish-shop. Mister Chop was a very black-looking man, so Jinks hoped he really was the sweep, though he kept a fish-shop that sold bread and cakes.

'Have you any soot for sale?' he asked the sweep.

'No, but I have plenty of bread,' said the sweep. 'If you want any soot, go and take it. There's some in a sack round the corner.'

Jinks told Tuppeny to get out and look. Soon Tuppeny came back with a small bag of very black soot.

'Put it in the back of the car under the seat,' said Jinks. So it was stowed away there.

Then Jinks drove straight towards a glittering palace that stood on a small hill in the distance. It was the right way up, which was curious to see in Topsy-Turvy Land. Jinks stopped the car behind a little group of big trees and jumped out. He opened his basket and made it into a tray. The little mouse was there as usual, sitting up and washing its whiskers. By it was a nice, new-laid brown egg.

'Just what I was looking for!' said Jinks, in delight. He took it out and put it into his pocket, very carefully. Then he shook a green cloak out of a brown parcel on the tray and a green hat to match.

'What are all those things for?' said Tuppeny, in surprise.

'You'll see!' grinned Jinks. He put on the green cloak, which had black cats embroidered all over it, and set the hat on his cheeky head. Then he took off his shoes and, to the other goblins' great surprise, emptied a great deal of soot into them. He gave them to Tuppeny to hold and told him to take great care of them and not drop them.

He put on a pair of slippers which he took from his tray. Then he swept his cloak around him and bowed grandly to Tuppeny and Feefo.

'Here you see before you, Minky-Monk, the Mighty Magician and his two goblin servants, come to pay a visit to his high-and-mightiness, the Topsy-Turvy Enchanter!' he chanted.

Tuppeny and Feefo stared at him as if he

really were quite mad. Jinks burst out laughing at their astonished faces.

'Don't look so surprised,' he said. 'I am just going to play a very simple trick on the Enchanter, that's all, and you must be my servants and help me.'

'We'll do our best,' said Feefo.

How the Great Enchanter was Captured

Leaving their car behind them, they set off up the hill to the palace, Feefo and Tuppeny holding up Jinks's cloak behind him for all the world as if he were very grand indeed.

Three heralds with silver trumpets stood at the gates of the palace, and when they saw the little procession coming they blew loud blasts on their trumpets in welcome. The glass door of the palace swung open in front of them and the three goblins marched inside.

What a strange sight met their wondering eyes! The ceiling of the palace hall was so high that it was lost in mist. Great glass pillars stood here and there, wreathed in strange, coloured flames that licked up and down the pillars all the time. The floor was black, so black that it seemed as if the goblins were walking on nothingness.

How the Great Enchanter was Captured

At the end of this hall was a high platform and on it a great glittering throne. Here sat Know-All, the Enchanter, King of Topsy-Turvy Land, but not at all topsy-turvy himself. His eyes were as sharp as needles, and his mouth was so thin that it looked like a thread of cotton.

'Here comes Minky-Monk, the Mighty Magician!' yelled Tuppeny, in his enormous voice. Jinks bowed deeply to the Enchanter, who nodded his head.

'Why do you come to me?' he asked, and his strange voice seemed to come from a hundred years away.

'I come to test your powers!' said Minky-Monk, boldly. 'I am a clever magician, some say even cleverer than you, and I have come to see what wonderful things you can do.'

'First show me what *you* can do!' said Know-All.

'Well, to begin with, I can easily do the three things I read on your proclamation,' said Jinks.

'Impossible!' said Know-All. 'No one can raise dust from the magic black stone in my palace garden – it is as hard as iron. And certainly none can show me anything never seen before, for I have lived a thousand years and in that time I have seen all there is to be seen,

and known all there is to be known. As for
reading my thoughts, such a thing could never be
done, for they are as secret as a cat's footfall!'

'I will strike dust from your black rock!'
cried Jinks. 'Come, let us go to it!'

The Enchanter arose and went down the
long, misty hall to the glass door. It swung
open and he and the goblins passed outside. A
vast black rock, whose surface was as smooth
as iron, stood within a grove of trees.

'There is the rock,' said Know-All. 'Stand
upon it, Magician, and see how vain are your
words!'

'Allow me to change my soft slippers for my shoes,' said Jinks, and slipped on his shoes carefully under his green cloak. Then he stepped on to the rock.

'Onnatipparootipoonaroryma!' he shouted, pretending that he was making a magic spell. He began to dance and jump about on the rock, and to the Enchanter's enormous surprise black dust flew out!

Tuppeny and Jinks turned away to hide their smiles. They knew it was only the soot in Jinks's shoes – but the Enchanter didn't! No, he stood there, with his mouth half open in wonder, and Jinks took the chance of kicking a cloud of soot towards him. Know-All shut his mouth with a snap, and began to cough and sneeze.

Jinks jumped and bounded, kicked and stamped all the harder till the air around was completely full of black dust, and Tuppeny and Feefo were coughing too.

'Enough, enough!' cried the Enchanter at last, seeing his hands and clothes getting black and dirty. 'I see you are very strong, Minky-Monk, and there is no doubt that you have kicked black dust from my magic rock.'

Jinks jumped down from the rock, very hot, and panted like a race-horse. They all returned to the palace and three servants took the goblins to three great bathrooms, where they bathed themselves and cleaned away the sticky soot.

Then back to the strange hall they went, staring in amazement at the flames that licked the glass pillars from top to bottom. The Enchanter was sitting on his throne, and as he was now quite clean the goblins thought he must have had a bath too!

'And now show me something that no one has ever seen before!' said Know-All.

'That's easy!' said Jinks, and he carefully took the brown egg out of his pocket. Know-All stared in amazement when he saw a hen's egg held out to him.

'Do you say that no one has ever seen that egg before?' he cried, scornfully. 'The hen has seen it – you have seen it – '

'Wait,' said Jinks. He suddenly crashed the egg on to the floor. It broke, and the yellow yolk streamed out.

'Tell me,' said Jinks, grinning. 'Has anyone in the world ever seen that yolk before, oh Enchanter?'

Know-All stared at it in anger. No, no one had ever seen that before, of course! It had been close-hidden in the shell, it could not be seen unless the egg was broken.

'This is but a trick,' said the Enchanter, harshly.

'No trick, but truth,' said Jinks, bowing.

Know-All sat silent for a moment. Then he spoke again, in his far-away voice.

'And now, oh very clever magician, tell me what I am thinking!'

Jinks stepped forward and looked into his deep eyes. 'You are thinking,' he said, 'you are thinking, oh Know-All, that I am Minky-Monk the Great Magician – but I am NOT! I am

Jinks, a sharp-witted goblin who is cleverer than you!'

Jinks threw off his green cloak and hat and stood before Know-All in his green suit and yellow stockings looking just what he was – a cheeky little green goblin.

The Enchanter leapt to his feet in surprise and rage. Thunder rolled through the palace and the flames that wreathed the pillars shot up higher than ever and changed to an angry red. Tuppeny and Feefo trembled, but Jinks stood unafraid.

For a moment the Enchanter seemed about to strike Jinks, to turn him into a beetle, to sweep him away to the moon, to do any one of the mighty things he was able to do. And then, very suddenly, seeing the goblin smiling there in front of him, he laughed.

'What's the use of being angry with a manni-kin like you!' he said. 'Yes, you are smart, you are sharp-witted, and I would dearly like to have you for my servant, though I should be afraid of you stealing my magic. But now, tremble, little goblin, for I will show you magi-cal things, things that will make you shiver and wish you had never come here to try your silly little tricks on me!'

'Great Enchanter, I ask for nothing better,'

cried Jinks, in a delighted voice. 'I have seen many great magicians and wizards perform their magic tricks, and if you can do better than they can, then indeed you will be clever. But I doubt it!'

The Enchanter took a thin silver stick and made three circles in the air, muttering as he did so. To the goblins' great astonishment he began to change! He grew an enormous spiked tail of a bright copper colour. His hands and feet changed to paws set with hundreds of claws – and then, before them was suddenly a giant dragon, almost filling the great hall, bellowing and roaring, sending flames and smoke out of his mouth!

'J-j-j-jumping b-b-beetles!' whispered Tuppeny, hiding under a chair. Feefo joined him – but Jinks stood watching the dragon, half afraid he was going to be eaten, but not daring to show his fear. The dragon suddenly dissolved into mist and out of it appeared the Enchanter again.

'What do you think of that?' he asked, proudly.

'Fairly good,' said Jinks. 'Not such a fierce dragon as I once saw the Green-eyed Witch change into, but still, not bad.'

The Enchanter went red with rage. He took up his silver stick again and waved it round

him. Immediately there appeared from the floor thousands of beautiful flowers growing and blossoming, sending out a very sweet scent. Jinks and the others gazed in delight. This was wonderful magic.

'Good,' said Jinks, at last. 'Quite good. I have never seen that done before in quite the same way.'

The garden vanished. The Enchanter glared at Jinks. He badly wanted to make him really astonished. He did not guess that the goblin was amazed already.

'You seem to think that everything I do is just ordinary,' he grumbled. 'Tell me something you would like me to do, and I will do it, no matter what it is! I will bring the moon down to the earth, fetch you a star, bring you the sea to my palace – only say what you wish, and I will do it.'

'Oh, don't do any of those things,' said Jinks, in alarm. 'I have found that it is the little, simple things that most wizards and enchanters cannot do.'

'Tell me one!' said the Enchanter.

'Well,' said Jinks, pretending to think hard, 'there is one thing that no one has ever shown me they can do yet – and that is, they can't turn themselves into a simple thing like a lump of sugar!'

'Easy!' shouted the Enchanter, scornfully. He picked up his silver stick and drew seven circles, each one smaller than the last, around him on the platform. Then he began to shrink very fast and to turn white. In two minutes' time there was a little white square thing in the middle of the smallest circle – a lump of white sugar.

Jinks, red with excitement, took a matchbox out of his pocket, emptied the matches on to the floor, made a dart at the piece of sugar, picked it up – and popped it into his match-box. He closed it quickly, and tied a piece of strong twine round and round it.

'Got him,' he said to the others, who were gaping at him in amazement.

'What do you mean, *got* him?' said Feefo.

'Well, haven't I got old Know-A-Lot as safe as can be?' said Jinks, doing a dance of joy. 'Isn't he in my match-box? He can't possibly get out, or make himself big because the match-box is very small and is tightly tied up. I can put him in my pocket and take him back to the King and Queen now!'

'Oh, Jinks, oh, Jinks, how clever, how wonderful you are!' cried Tuppeny and Feefo in joy.

The lump of sugar began to rattle about in the box and a high voice called out, 'What have you done to me? Open the box at once and let me go back to my own shape, or I will turn you into a spotted frog!'

'You just try!' said Jinks, cheerfully. 'If you get up to any tricks, Enchanter, I shall pop you into some warm water and let you melt away and that will be the end of you!'

'Come on,' said Tuppeny, pulling at Jinks's sleeve. 'Let's go. I don't much like this palace. Look at the flames on those pillars. They seem as if they are trying to put out hot tongues to reach us.'

How the Great Enchanter was Captured

Jinks took a look and then quickly ran out of the palace. No sooner had the goblins gone outside than there came a rumbling sound, and the whole palace went up in green flames! Nothing was left of it – not even a chair.

'That was a narrow escape,' said Jinks,

looking pale. 'Come on, let's get to our car.'

They ran to their car, jumped into it and set off hurriedly through the Land of Topsy-Turvy, not stopping for anything or anyone, not even for a policeman who wore a helmet on his feet and shouted strange, angry things to them.

They came to the Grumbling Wood and went through it as quickly as they could, and at last through the Land of Night. They were very glad when they saw the pretty toadstool houses of the Pixie-Folk.

Tiptoe was standing at their gate, watching for them. She waved in delight when she saw them coming up the lane.

'But where's the Enchanter?' she said, in disappointment, when she saw there was no one with them.

'Here!' said Jinks, and rattled his match-box.

'Whatever do you mean?' said Tiptoe. 'Let me see.'

'Oh, no!' said Jinks. 'If I let him out I really don't know *what* would happen. I'm just going off to the King and Queen to give him to them.'

The three jumped into their car and drove at top speed to the King's palace. They were shown into the King's presence at once, and the Queen came hurrying in when she heard the three goblins were there.

'Success, Your Majesties!' said Jinks, bowing low, and presenting the match-box to the King. 'Inside is a lump of white sugar – the Enchanter. If you want to get rid of him, put him into warm water and let him melt away.'

'Ow-ooh-ah!' yelled the Enchanter in the match-box, almost beside himself with fear and rage. 'Set me free, oh King, and I will do anything you please.'

'Don't listen to him,' said Jinks, earnestly. 'Make him do all you want, Your Majesty, and then decide what you will do with him.

The King and Queen were delighted and truly amazed. They listened to Jinks's story of the capture in admiration and praised the clever goblin highly.

'You shall have that palace over there, if you like,' said the King, and the goblins, looking out of the window, saw a fine palace glittering in the sunshine.

'Thank you,' said Jinks, bowing again. 'Do tell me what you are going to do about the Enchanter.'

'First he will have to bring back all the fairies

and elves he has spirited away,' said the King.
'Then he will have to put right all the harm
and wrong he has done. Then, if he is still bent
on wickedness, we shall melt him away – but
if not, we may give him another chance.'

'Good, Your Majesty!' said Jinks. 'Now, if
we may, we will leave you and go home.'

'Goodbye and very many thanks,' said the
King, putting the match-box into his pocket.
'Take the palace whenever you like.'

Off went the goblins, talking at top speed.
A palace of their own! Ooh!

How the Great Enchanter was Captured

'But, you know,' said Feefo, sensibly, 'a palace costs a great deal to run, what with servants and all that sort of thing. I think we had better let it to a prince or someone like that till we've enough money ourselves.'

'Oh, yes!' said Tuppeny, delighted. 'You know, Jinks, I do love our little cottage so much. I'm sure I should be homesick if we lived in the palace. Let's wait till we're very, very rich.'

Then off they went back to Hollyhock Cottage, anxious to tell Tiptoe about their palace – but, dear me, *how* pleased she was to hear that they were still going to live next door to her, after all!

The Adventure of the Surprising Blue Tablecloth

One day, when the goblins were out to tea with Tiptoe, and eating a lovely new chocolate cake made that morning, there came a knock at her door. Tiptoe went to answer it and gave a cry of surprise.

'Uncle Hoppetty! How nice to see you! Do come and have tea. There's a nice new chocolate cake.'

'Who are all these people?' asked Uncle Hoppetty, looking round at the three goblins, who had at once got up and bowed politely to the twinkling-eyed old man. He wasn't much bigger than they were, but he was very broad. His eyes were very blue and twinkled like stars on a frosty night.

'These are my great friends, Tuppeny, Jinks, and Feefo,' said Tiptoe. 'You must have heard of them, Uncle Hoppetty. They have just been clever enough to capture the great Enchanter Know-All for their Majesties, the King and Queen.'

'Bewhisker me! Is that really so!' said Tiptoe's uncle in surprise and admiration. 'Pleased to meet you, young men! Dear, dear, to think of meeting you here! Do tell me some of your adventures!'

So the three goblins took it in turn to tell all they had done, and Uncle Hoppetty listened in astonishment. Suddenly he banged his fist on the table, and cried:

'Bewhisker me! Have you ever heard of the Wonderful Tablecloth owned by Nobbly the Gnome? You really ought to go and get it!'

'Tell us about it,' begged Jinks.

'Well, this Tablecloth, which is as blue as the sky, is very magic,' said Hoppetty. 'No sooner do you spread it on a table and say 'Cloth, give me breakfast,' or 'Cloth, give me dinner,' than it at once covers itself with the most delicious dishes of all kinds for you to eat. I expect you have heard tales of it before. It was lost for many years and then Nobbly found it somewhere.'

'But wouldn't we have to pay a lot for it?' asked Feefo, doubtfully.

'That's just what I was coming to,' said
Uncle Hoppetty, his bright eyes shining. 'I
happen to know that Nobbly's house is falling
down and he doesn't want to build another one.
He has always longed to live in a palace – so,
as you don't want to live in *your* palace just yet,
why don't you go to Nobbly and offer him your
palace in exchange for his Tablecloth? I've no
doubt he is tired of it by now.'

'I say!' said Jinks, rubbing his hands

together in delight. 'Wouldn't it be fine to have a cloth like that? No more cooking! No more marketing! Ooh!'

'We'd ask you to tea every Friday,' said Tuppeny to Uncle Hoppetty.

'Bewhisker me! That's a fine idea!' said Hoppetty at once. He really did love a good meal.

'We'll do it!' said Feefo, making a noise like ten cats, purring for joy.

Uncle Hoppety looked round the kitchen in astonishment. 'Where's that cat?' he said to Tiptoe. 'I didn't know you had one.'

'There it is!' said Tiptoe, pointing to the grinning Feefo. 'Stop purring, Feefo, and pass the biscuits.'

It was soon settled that the very next day the goblins should set off to the Nobbly Gnome's and offer him the loan of their palace for his wonderful Tablecloth. The gnome didn't live very far away – only about eight hours' drive in the little green car – so if they started off in the morning, they could spend the night somewhere on the way back and arrive home the day after.

They cleaned up their car and Tiptoe packed sandwiches for them, and what was left of the chocolate cake. They set off at seven o'clock in the morning, when the silvery mist hung over the fields, and everything was very beautiful. Tiptoe wished she were coming with them, it was such a lovely day.

'Good-bye, good-bye!' she cried. 'Take care of yourselves, goblins, and come back safely with the Blue Tablecloth.'

'Of course!' shouted all three together, and then Feefo made a noise like fifty hooters honking, which made Jinks jump so much that he nearly drove the car into the hedge.

'Don't do that!' he said, fiercely. 'Or else, if you do, just warn me first.'

They drove on through villages and countrysides, through big goblin-towns, full of all kinds and colours of goblins, shouting, buying, selling. Some of them knew the three green goblins, but Jinks didn't stop.

They had their sandwich lunch in a little sunny dell by the side of a lane, and drank from a clear, bubbling brook near by. Then they packed themselves into the car again and once more set off for the Nobbly Gnome's.

They came to his town at last, and asked for his house. It was a large one, painted bright yellow, and it was certainly falling to bits.

One of the chimneys had gone, and part of the roof had fallen in, so that the rain fell through and wetted everything.

The goblins got out of their car and went to the door. The bell was broken and there was no knocker, so they had to rap with their fists.

'Come in, come in, come in!' shouted a voice, and Jinks pushed open the door. The goblins went inside and found themselves in a room, perfectly round, with a big fire burning in the middle. The Nobbly Gnome was sitting over it, reading a large book. He wore four pairs of spectacles on his nose and two on his forehead, so he really looked very funny.

'What do you want?' he asked, looking over the top of his four pairs of spectacles in rather a cross way.

'We've come to see if you'd like to live in a palace on a hill that belongs to us,' said Jinks. 'Your house seems to be falling down. It might fall on your head one day and that would be the end of you.'

'Stars and moon, do you really think it might?' cried the startled gnome, looking up at the ceiling nervously. 'Well, I've always wanted to live in a palace, and I'm sure it's very kind of you to offer me yours. I suppose you want something in return?'

'Well, we do rather,' said Jinks. 'We heard

you had a wonderful cloth that could bring any meal you wished for. Could you spare us that cloth, do you think, in exchange for the loan of our palace?'

'Certainly!' said the Nobbly Gnome, shutting up his book and sliding the two odd pairs of spectacles down on to his nose with the others. 'I'm tired of the cloth, you know. I've had it for about seventy years and I know all the breakfasts, dinners, teas and suppers it's got. I'll give it to you with the greatest pleasure, if you'll be kind enough to lend me your palace. Do you know if there is hot and cold water in all the bedrooms of your palace?'

'Sure to be,' said Jinks. 'It's quite a new one. You can wash yourself in every room if you like.'

'That really will be exciting,' beamed the gnome, who certainly looked as if he could do with a wash in some sort of basin. 'I have to pump my own water here, and as I always forget I can hardly ever wash.'

'No wonder you look a bit dir – ' began Tuppeny, but Feefo nudged him hard and he just stopped in time.

'Don't annoy him!' whispered Feefo. 'Nobody likes being called dirty.'

'Have you got the Tablecloth handy?' asked Jinks.

'Well – not exactly handy,' said the Nobbly Gnome, pushing all his spectacles back on to his forehead and looking round the kitchen. 'Let me see now. You might look in that cupboard over there. I believe I put it there when I filled the kitchen drawer full of mousetraps. My larder was full of mice, you know, and I really had to get some traps.'

'Did you catch many mice?' asked Jinks, politely, as he went to the cupboard.

'Well, no,' said the Nobbly Gnome. 'I forgot to set the traps, really, but I'm sure I should have caught hundreds if I hadn't forgotten.'

'It's not in the cupboard,' said Jinks. 'The cupboard is simply full of bottles of vinegar.'

'Dear me, so that was where the vinegar went to!' said the Nobbly Gnome in surprise. 'You know, I had a tremendous lot of onions in my garden last year, and I bought all those bottles of vinegar to pickle them. I couldn't think where I'd put the vinegar, so the onions were all wasted. It was such a pity.'

The three goblins stared at the gnome in astonishment. What a forgetter he was!

'Well, do you know where you put the Magic Cloth after you took it out of the cupboard to make room for the vinegar bottles?' said Jinks.

'Let me see now – yes, you might look in

the wood-box under the sink,' said the gnome, thinking hard. 'I often stuff things there to put them out of the way.'

'I think you ought to have been more careful of such a wonderful thing as that Tablecloth,' said Feefo, and the gnome looked half ashamed of himself.

'I was very careful of it when it gave me my meals,' he said, 'but after that it was just a nuisance.'

Tuppeny found the wood-box under the sink and took off the lid. It was full of shirts and socks, but there was no Blue Tablecloth there!

'Bless me!' said the gnome, in surprise, 'so that's where last week's laundry went to! Of course, I remember now! The boy wanted the laundry basket back, so I emptied everything out of the wood-box and stuffed my clean shirts and socks there. Well, well, I can put on a clean pair of socks now.'

'Yes, but where did you put the *TABLE-CLOTH?*' shouted Jinks, feeling that he might lose his temper at any moment.

'Oh, bother that wretched Tablecloth!' said the gnome, frowning. 'Don't I *keep* remembering where it is?'

'No, you keep remembering where it *isn't!*' said Jinks, sharply. 'Now, think hard, Nobbly Gnome. Where did you put it after you had taken it out of the wood-box?'

'I put it – I put it – in that big green teapot up on the dresser,' said the Nobbly Gnome, polishing up all his pairs of spectacles in a vexed manner.

'In the *tea*pot!' said all the goblins, in surprise. 'But whatever for?'

'Well, you must put things somewhere, mustn't you?' said the gnome, in a grumpy voice. 'And I never do use that teapot. It's much too big. It would do nicely for a hippopotamus.'

Feefo at once made a noise like a hippo and the Nobbly Gnome gave a shriek and disappeared under the sofa.

'Don't be silly, Feefo,' said Jinks in despair. 'If you frighten him, he'll never remember anything at all. Fancy snorting like a hippo at an important time like this!'

Feefo stopped at once and went to the dresser where a giant-size teapot stood. He took it down and looked into it.

'There's no Blue Tablecloth here!' he said, in disgust. 'It's full of pearls!'

'Just fancy that now!' said the Nobbly Gnome. 'I wondered where I had put all my cat's pearls.'

'Your cat's pearls!' said Jinks. 'What next!'

'Oh, haven't you heard about my cat?' asked the gnome, in surprise. 'He's a marvellous cat. When he purrs, big pearls drop out of his mouth. I used to collect them and make them into necklaces for my friends, then I got tired of it. I emptied the pearls out of their box into that teapot the other day. I remember quite clearly now.'

'And what did you do with the Tablecloth, when you took it out of the teapot to make room for the pearls?' asked Jinks, patiently, beginning to feel this must be a most annoying sort of dream.

'I really don't know,' said the gnome, help-lessly, looking round. 'Oh, look – there it is, hanging up by the sink, under our noses all the time!'

'Where?' said all the goblins, excitedly, look-ing at the sink.

'Why, that cloth there,' said the gnome, pointing to a grey and dirty dishcloth hanging on a nail.

'That *dish*cloth!' said Jinks, in horror. 'Do you mean to say you used that Magic Table-cloth for a *dish*cloth, Nobbly Gnome? How *could* you do such a thing?'

'Well, I must have *some*thing for a dishcloth, mustn't I?' grumbled the gnome. '*I* don't know where all my dishcloths have gone to. I had dozens.'

'They are probably in the dustbin, I should think,' said Jinks, going over to get the dirty cloth. He took some soap, pumped some water into a bowl and began to wash the cloth. It came a beautiful blue colour when it was clean. Jinks shook it out – and Tuppeny gave a shriek.

'Jinks! There's only half of it! Look!'

Sure enough it had been torn in half. You could see the ragged edge plainly.

'Is it any good when it is torn in half?' asked Jinks.

'Oh, no, none,' said the Nobbly Gnome, cheerfully. 'Yes, I remember tearing it in half now. I wanted the other piece to clean my boots with.'

Jinks groaned. He had certainly only just come to the rescue of the Tablecloth in time! It was Tuppeny who found the boot-box – and inside, for a wonder, was the other half of the Blue Tablecloth. It took a very long time to get it clean, for it was covered with black polish.

When both halves were clean and dry, Jinks hunted for a needle and cotton. There didn't seem to be such a thing in the Nobbly Gnome's house.

'And if there is, it won't be in the work-basket,' said Jinks. 'It will be in the kettle or somewhere like that!'

In the end Jinks opened his basket and from his tray took a reel of cotton and a packet of needles. Then he neatly sewed the two halves of the cloth together. It was mended!

'Now let's see it work!' said Tuppeny, excited.

The Nobbly Gnome took it and spread it smoothly on his table.

51

'Cloth, give us a good, late tea!' he commanded.

Wonder of wonders! Marvels of marvels! On to that bright blue cloth appeared two new loaves of crusty bread, a big dish of golden butter, a great jar of golden honey, one big fruit cake, a large dish of sardines in oil, a flat dish of delicious ham, a cold chicken and a steaming pot of sweet cocoa. Think of that!

'Ooh! This is the only sensible thing you've done so far!' said Tuppeny, hungrily, slapping the Nobbly Gnome on the back.

They all sat down and made an excellent

meal. It was half-past six and they were very hungry indeed.

'I'm sorry I can't ask you to stay here for the night,' said Nobbly, afterwards. 'But to tell you the truth, I've put my bed somewhere and I can't think where, so I only have a sofa to sleep on myself. But if you drive on for forty miles you'll come to an inn called "Welcome," and the landlord will be pleased to put you up, I'm sure.'

'Thank you,' said Jinks, getting up from the table. 'What do we do with all the remains of our tea?'

'Oh, just this,' said Nobbly, and he gave the cloth a tug. Immediately all the dishes disappeared, and the cloth was clean and bare. Nobbly folded it up, and gave it to Jinks, who put it safely into his biggest pocket.

'I suppose you wouldn't like to come with us, would you?' he asked the Gnome. 'We can't very well bring your palace to you, you see. You'll have to come and see it.'

'Oh, I'd love to!' cried Nobbly, joyfully. So they all packed themselves into the car, though it was a bit of a squeeze with four of them, and Jinks drove off through the night.

They arrived at the Welcome Inn at last and

Jinks hammered on the door, which was fast-shut.

'Who's there?' said a gruff voice, and a big head looked out of a window.

'Guests!' said Jinks. 'We want to stay the night.'

'I've no food for you and but one bed,' said the surly voice.

'Oh, never mind,' said Jinks, impatiently. 'We are tired. Let us in. Why do you call your inn "Welcome," if you greet your guests in this way?'

With a great deal of mumbling and grumbling the landlord came heavily down the stairs and unbolted the door. The goblins and the gnome stepped inside and shivered, for the inn was very cold and damp. They saw the glint of a fire in one room and went there.

'There's no food in the house, as I told you,' said the landlord.

'Don't worry, we've plenty for ourselves,' said Jinks, thinking of the Blue Tablecloth he had in his pocket.

'Is it out in your car then?' asked the landlord, seeing they had nothing with them. 'Shall I tell my servant to fetch it in for you?'

'No thanks, we've got it with us,' said Jinks, much to the landlord's amazement.

'There's a big bed in the next room,' said he. 'You can sleep there when you are ready. Good night to you.'

'Good night!' said everyone, and he went stumping out of the room.

The Black Cat and the Red Whip

'I don't like the landlord very much,' said Tuppeny.

'I've a good mind to make a noise like twenty more people arriving, and give him a fright,' chuckled Feefo.

'No, don't,' said Nobbly in alarm. 'He might turn us out and I'm *so* sleepy.'

'Anybody want a cup of hot milk and some biscuits before we go to bed?' asked Jinks, shaking out his wonderful Tablecloth and spreading it on the table.

'I'd like some milk and some chocolate biscuits,' cried Tuppeny at once.

'And I'll have some supper too!' said Feefo.

'Cloth, give us a light supper,' commanded Jinks. At once the cloth spread itself with a big jug of hot milk, two plates of sweet biscuits and a dish of small buns. All the goblins and the gnome helped themselves in delight – and not one of them saw the landlord peeping in amazement through the crack in the half-open door!

'So that's what they meant when they said they had their food with them!' he thought to himself. 'My, if I had that cloth, what fortunes I would make! I'd never need to go marketing, I'd never need to cook or bake. Everything I wanted I could get from that cloth.'

After a little while Jinks tugged the cloth and the remains of their supper vanished. He put it back into his pocket and they all four of them went into the next room. The bed was a big one, so they climbed into it and lay down comfortably in a row. Jinks was on the outside, Tuppeny and Feefo in the middle, and Nobbly by the wall, because he was so afraid of falling out.

Soon they were all asleep, tired out with their exciting day – and when little snores and snorts came from the bedroom, the big landlord crept through the door in his bare feet. The moon shone into the room and he saw that Jinks lay on the outside. That was lucky. He saw a corner of the Blue Tablecloth hanging out of the goblin's pocket and he gave it a gentle pull.

A little of it came out – then a little more. Jinks didn't stir. He always slept very soundly

indeed. The landlord pulled again – and in a few minutes' time he had managed to get the whole of the cloth into his hands.

He stole out of the room. He lighted a lamp and looked at the cloth. Had he got one like it in his linen chest?

He took the lamp and went to look. He pulled out white cloths, green ones, orange ones – and then two blue ones. One of them was a bright blue, almost like the Magic Cloth. The landlord tore it in half and neatly mended it again, just as he saw had been done to the Magic Cloth. Then he stole back to the bedroom and pushed his cloth gently into Jinks's pocket.

In the morning the three goblins and the gnome awoke and yawned. At first they wondered where they were, but very soon they remembered. They jumped out of bed, washed themselves out in the yard at the pump, and then went into the inn to pay the landlord and to have their breakfast.

Jinks shook out the cloth and spread it on a table. 'Cloth, give us a good breakfast,' he commanded. Everyone looked hungrily to see what sort of breakfast was going to appear. Eggs and bacon? Porridge and treacle? Kippers and toast?

The cloth lay there quite empty! Not a dish came, not a tiny piece of toast. Jinks stared in surprise. Then he spoke again. 'Come, come,

Cloth, give us a good breakfast and be quick
about it!'

But no – the cloth wouldn't do a thing. It
just behaved like an ordinary tablecloth and the
goblins were most disappointed and amazed.

'Is it *my* cloth?' asked Nobbly, at last.

'Yes, look – here's the place where it was
torn down the middle and I mended it,' said
Jinks.

'I expect tearing it in half like that and using
it for a dishcloth and a polishing rag has spoilt
the magic,' said Feefo, gloomily. 'It just did a
bit of magic yesterday, but I expect that's all
it will do now. You ought to be ashamed of
yourself, Nobbly Gnome, for using a wonderful
thing like that in such wrong ways.'

'Shan't I get your palace now?' asked
Nobbly, pushing all his spectacles up on to his
head in despair.

'Of course not,' said Jinks. 'Unless you've
anything else to give us in exchange that is as
good as this cloth was.'

'Well – there's my cat,' said Nobbly. 'Would
he do, do you think? He purrs pearls beautifully, you know.'

The three goblins cheered up at once. A cat
that purred pearls would be almost better than
a cloth that gave free meals!

'Yes, that would do,' said Jinks. 'Come on, let's drive back to your house, Nobbly, and get the cat.'

So back they went to Nobbly's house.

'Anyway, thank goodness the cat's alive and can't be put into all sorts of silly places like the cloth was,' said Feefo when they arrived.

'And can't be cut in half and used for a dishcloth,' said Tuppeny.

'Don't scold me so,' said Nobbly. 'If you do, I shall forget what the cat's name is and it will only come if it is called by its right name.'

'Jumping beetles!' groaned Tuppeny. 'Don't say you're going to forget the cat's name, Nobbly.'

'Well, I'm not quite sure, but I think it's something to do with a chimney,' said Nobbly, after thinking hard for a few minutes.

'Something to do with a chimney, Nobbly!' said Jinks. 'You must be mad.'

'A roof has to do with a chimney,' said Feefo. 'Perhaps the cat's name is Rufus.'

'Rufus, Rufus, Rufus!' shouted Jinks, at once. But no cat came.

'Perhaps it's a name *like* chimney,' said Tuppeny. 'Timmy or Bimmy, or something like that.'

61

So they tried Timmy and Bimmy, and Jimmy too, but no cat came at all.

'Try to think of its name again,' begged the goblin – but all Nobbly could say was that its name reminded him of chimneys.

'What's the cat like?' asked Tuppeny.

'Oh, as black as a sweep,' said Nobbly.

'Sweep, Sweep, Sweep!' called Tuppeny. No answer from any cat at all.

'Make a noise like cream being poured into a saucer, Feefo,' begged Jinks, suddenly. So Feefo pursed up his lips and made a thick, creamy, delicious sort of noise, which made everyone think of a jugful of cream being poured slowly into a saucer.

That did the trick! At once a large black cat came running in at the kitchen door, mewing loudly.

'Oh, look, here's Sooty!' shouted Nobbly in delight.

'Sooty! Is that his name?' said Jinks.

'Of course!' said Nobbly.

'Well, why couldn't you think of it before?' said Feefo. 'Making us waste all this time!'

'I always think of Sooty's name when I *see* him,' said Nobbly, 'but never when he isn't there. I just think of chimneys or something then.'

'Of course! Sooty chimneys!' said Jinks, with a groan. 'You've just got the most upside-down brains ever I knew, Nobbly. You'd be at home in Topsy-Turvy Land! It's a pity our palace isn't there.'

'Let's see the cat purr pearls,' said Feefo.

So Nobbly stroked the big cat, and when it began to purr, what a strange thing! Creamy pearls fell from its mouth and rolled about the floor. The goblins watched in delight.

They spent the day at Nobbly's, for he was anxious to pack up some of his books to take to the palace, and it took a long time to find them. But at last they were all in the car and the four of them set off again, the cat sitting on Nobbly's shoulder.

'We'll have to spend the night at the same inn,' said Jinks. 'And the landlord will have to give us a meal this time, for our wonderful cloth no longer works!'

The landlord was surprised to see them, but he let them come in. They took the cat in with them, and it sat silent by the fire.

'We haven't our food with us this time,' said Jinks. 'You must get us some.' The landlord said he would, and went away. He returned with a good supper, and asked the goblins to pay him.

'We haven't the money to pay you now,' said Jinks, feeling in his pocket. 'Would you accept a few pearls instead?'

'Certainly,' said the landlord, in surprise. He made up his mind to watch where these strange little visitors got their pearls from – and when he saw them stroking the cat, which let pearls fall from its mouth as it purred, he was more

astonished than when he had seen the wonderful cloth!

He glued his eye to the crack in the door,
and marvelled. Could he steal that cat too? It
should be easy enough!

When the goblins and the gnome were
asleep, the landlord crept to the bedroom. The
cat lay at the foot of the bed, awake. It was
listening for mice.

'Mouse!' whispered the landlord. 'Mouse!'

At once Sooty jumped off the bed and ran
to the door. The landlord popped him into a
large bag he had ready and tiptoed away at
once. He looked at the cat closely when he was
in his room and saw that it was black all over
except for a little piece under its chest, which
was white.

'Just like my old stable cat!' he chuckled.
'I'll go and get her!'

Out he went and soon tempted the stable cat
to come to him by dangling a herring behind
him on a string. He caught her and took her
to the goblins' bedroom. He shut her in there
with them and went off to bed, delighted with
his evening's work.

The next day, what a commotion when the
goblins found that the cat wouldn't give them
a single pearl! They stroked her gently, they

stroked her hard – she purred as loudly as she could, surprised at all the attention she was getting. But she was only an ordinary stable cat and no matter how she purred, no pearls fell from her whiskered mouth!

'I suppose your cat's no use away from home,' said Jinks, at last. 'It's most disappointing, really. Now whatever are we to do?'

'Have you anything else magic?' asked Feefo.

'Only a red whip,' said poor Nobbly. 'You can have that if you like.'

So back to his house they went, and wonder

66

of wonders, they found the Red Whip almost
at once! It actually stood in the right place –
in the umbrella stand!

'What does it do?' asked Jinks, taking it out
and looking at it.

'It just whips people who are my enemies,'
said Nobbly. 'It isn't very magic, I'm afraid.
If a burglar came in the night it would hop out
of the umbrella-stand and whip him till he went
away.'

'Well, it doesn't sound as if it would be much
use to us,' said Jinks, doubtfully.

'Can't I have your palace then?' said poor
disappointed Nobbly, his eyes filling with tears.
Tuppeny was upset to see him unhappy and
put his arms round him.

'Jinks, do let him have our palace,' he
begged. 'After all, he was quite willing for us
to have his Tablecloth and his Cat, and he
couldn't help it if the magic went out of them.'

'All right,' said Jinks, at once. 'Cheer up,
Nobbly Gnome. You can have our palace for a
year at any rate. And if we manage to sell your
Red Whip to anyone you can have the palace
for longer.'

'Oh, thank you!' said Nobbly, quite cheered
up. 'Well, shall we start off now?'

'We might as well,' said Jinks. 'We could

get to Heyho Village by this evening if we set off now. We don't need to stop at that horrid Welcome Inn again then.'

'Come on,' said Feefo, clucking like a hen for joy, and making Nobbly look everywhere to see where the chicken was. He never could get used to Feefo's noises.

'What about the cat?' said Tuppeny. 'It came back with us in the car. It's rather a nice cat and it's a shame to leave it here all by itself. It might starve. We'd better take it with us. It might suddenly get its magic back again. You never know!'

'Yes, let's take it,' said Jinks. 'Where did it go when it got out of the car?'

Nobody had noticed.

'And I've forgotten its name again,' said Nobbly in dismay.

'Well, *we* haven't!' said Feefo at once. 'Our brains aren't quite so muddled as yours, Nobbly. Now think – it's something to do with chimneys!'

But poor old Nobbly could *not* remember the name.

'You have a most wonderful forgettery!' said Feefo. 'Now, where's that cat? Sooty, Sooty, Sooty!'

No cat appeared.

'That's funny,' said Nobbly, puzzled. 'Sooty always comes when his name is called. Always!'

'SOOTY, SOOTY, SOOTY!' yelled Tuppeny in his most enormous voice, and startled Nobbly so much that he sat down suddenly in a basin of potatoes that he had stupidly left on a chair behind him.

'I wondered where I had left those potatoes,' he said, drying himself. Tuppeny shrieked with laughter, and Jinks and Feefo both thought that really Nobbly was quite mad.

'Where *is* that cat!' said Jinks, crossly. 'If we don't find it we shall never start off in time to get to Heyho Village today.'

But, you know, they didn't find the cat, and it wouldn't even answer when they called 'Sooty, Sooty!' Nor would it come even when Feefo made a noise like cream being poured out, again, which was really very extraordinary, Nobbly thought.

'Well, we can't wait any longer,' said Jinks.

'I'm awfully hungry,' said Tuppeny.

'So am I,' said Feefo. 'Hadn't we better have dinner before we start, Jinks?'

'All right,' said Jinks, sighing. 'But that means we shan't get home tonight. We shall have to stay at that horrid inn again.'

They found some sardines and bought some

bread and some butter. Jinks took some chocolate and apples out of his wonderful basket so they made quite a good meal. Then they all packed themselves into the car again and set off.

But it was an unlucky day for them. The little car got a bad puncture and it took Jinks a long time to get the wheel off and the spare wheel on. It was past tea-time before they could start again, and just as it was getting dark they drew up at the Welcome Inn.

The landlord gaped in surprise to see the little party again, and welcomed them more heartily than he had done before, for he felt sure that they would have something valuable that he might steal again.

'Bring us supper,' said Jinks, flinging his hat down on a table. 'We are hungry, so please be quick.'

'I say! We've left that Red Whip out in the car!' whispered Tuppeny to Jinks. Jinks went out at once to fetch it and brought it back. The landlord watched him and made up his mind that he would peep through the crack of the door and see what the whip did for the goblins and the gnome.

'Maybe it cracks out gold for them!' he thought to himself.

He took in a fine supper, which he had got from the Magic Tablecloth, and he was careful to lock up the black cat so that it would not go near his guests. Then he put his eye to the crack in the door to watch what the Red Whip did.

But to his great disappointment it did nothing at all! Jinks stood it by his chair whilst

71

he ate his supper, and took no further notice of it.

'We'll go to bed now,' he said, when they had all finished. 'Then we can get up early in the morning and get to Heyho Village in good time. Tiptoe will be wondering whatever has become of us!'

So off they went to lie in the big bed. Jinks took the Red Whip with him and stood it at the head of the bed. The landlord watched him and felt perfectly certain that the Whip was magic in some way. He would steal it that very night! There was an old whip in the stables he could dip into a pot of red paint and put into its place.

So, when the goblins and the gnome lay fast asleep, the landlord crept once more into their bedroom. He tiptoed to the head of the bed and put out his hand for the Whip. But, strange to say, it dodged to one side!

'Oho!' said the landlord, pleased to find it was magic, just as he had thought. 'So you *are* magic, are you!'

He made another grab at it – and then the Whip did an even stranger thing. It gave a loud crack and struck the surprised landlord on the back.

'Ow!' he yelled, jumping three feet into the

air with fright and pain. The Whip gave another loud crack and hit the frightened man once more. He yelled in horror – and, of course, all the goblins and the gnome woke up in a hurry! Jinks lighted the lamp – and what a strange sight he saw!

The Whip was whipping the landlord all round the room! He ran out into the passage and the Whip followed him, whipping away for all it was worth! The landlord yelled and the Whip cracked so there was a fine old noise.

'Shall I stop the Whip?' said Nobbly, anxiously.

'No,' said Jinks, a curious look coming over his face. 'No. That landlord must have come into our room to steal something or the Whip wouldn't have attacked him. Let it go on whipping him and see what he says.'

The landlord rushed into their room, crying big tears. The Whip followed, slashing away at his broad shoulders.

'Mercy, mercy!' begged the landlord, falling on his knees. 'Mercy, kind sirs!'

'What were you doing in our room?' asked Jinks, sternly.

'Nothing, nothing!' wept the landlord. At this the Whip attacked him all the more and he yelled with pain.

'Confess everything and we will stop the Whip from beating you!' said Jinks.

'I will tell you all,' sobbed the landlord, now almost frightened out of his wits. 'It was I who took your cloth and put another in its place. It was I who stole your cat and gave you my stable cat instead. I came to steal your whip tonight, but it set upon me like this.'

The goblins and the gnome listened in the greatest amazement and disgust. So that was what had happened! No wonder the cloth and the cat would not give out their magic any more!

'Get us the cloth and the cat at once,' said Jinks. The landlord got up and staggered off, the Whip dancing nimbly round him and getting in a few good cuts whenever it saw a chance. Ah, truly the thief of a landlord was getting his punishment now!

He came back with the cloth in one hand and the cat in another.

'Sooty, Sooty!' cried Feefo. The cat purred with delight and at once pearls fell from its mouth. Jinks took the cloth, spread it and commanded it to give them a meal. At once it became covered with delicious dishes of food. It was the Magic Tablecloth, there was no doubt about it.

'Make the Whip stop beating me,' begged the landlord. 'I have given you back all I stole.'

'Whip, stop your antics and go back to Jinks,' commanded Nobbly. The Whip at once jumped into Jinks's hand and stood there quietly.

'You have had a good punishment for your dishonesty,' said Jinks, severely. 'See that you treat your guests fairly and honestly in future, for if I ever hear that you have been dishonest again I will send my Whip to you at once.'

'I will never rob anyone again,' wept the scared landlord. 'Oh, forgive me, and take your Whip away when you go tomorrow.'

The next morning the goblins and the gnome packed the cat, the cloth and the whip into their car, called out a last warning to the frightened landlord, who could hardly walk that morning, he was so stiff with his beating, and set off for Heyho Village.

'At last!' said Jinks. 'I began to think we should never get home again!'

'I'm getting so excited about my palace,' said Nobbly, rubbing his hands together. 'If you like you can have all three of my magic things, Jinks. I think they would be safer with you than with me. I can always borrow them if I want them.

'Of course!' said Jinks. 'You may be sure *we* shan't use the cloth as a dishcloth or a polishing rag, Nobbly, and none of us will forget Sooty's name!'

Sooty purred and a dozen pearls trickled down Nobbly's neck, for the cat was sitting on his shoulder as usual.

'Ooh!' he said, wriggling. 'Don't do that, Sooty. It tickles me.'

How pleased Tiptoe was to see them all! She and Uncle Hoppetty were waiting anxiously for them, and when they saw all the magic things they had with them, how surprised and delighted they were! As for Nobbly he nearly fell over himself with delight when he saw his palace!

'It's grand, it's grand, it's grand!' he sang, going into all the bedrooms and turning on the taps.

'Just you remember to turn them off again!' called Jinks, when the goblins left the gnome. 'Or you'll find you've got a swimming-pool instead of a palace!'

Then off they went to Hollyhock Cottage, chuckling loudly whenever they thought of dear old Nobbly and his upside-down brains!

The Lost Princess and the Bewitched Tree

One morning, when Jinks and Feefo were eating a good breakfast given to them by the Magic Tablecloth and Tuppeny was giving the black cat some milk in a saucer, there came the sound of someone running quickly up the path to the front door. Then little hands knocked on the door and a voice cried 'Oh, quick, quick, help me!'

Jinks leapt up and rushed to the door. He opened it and there stood the prettiest little pixie girl you could imagine! Her hair was as black as a rook's wing, and as curly as a lamb's coat. Her eyes were the colour of brown brooks and her face was like a flower.

But she was crying bitterly! Jinks took her hands and pulled her indoors. 'What's the matter?' he asked.

'Oh, green goblin, my sister has been stolen away!' sobbed the pixie. 'I'm the Princess

Lightfoot and my sister is the Princess Light-heart. Oh, please, please do find her for me.'

'Tell me how she was stolen,' said Jinks.

'Well, we were out in the woods,' said Light-foot. 'Lightheart is good at climbing trees – so she thought she would climb a tall one, right to the very top. She climbed up and up, and I watched her – but oh dear, oh dear, when she reached the top, she disappeared!'

'Jumping beetles!' said Tuppeny in surprise. He couldn't take his eyes off the pretty little pixie. He couldn't bear to see her crying. He felt he wanted to put his arms round her and love her.

'Don't cry!' said fat little Tuppeny, pushing forward. '*I'll* rescue your sister for you!'

Jinks and Feefo were surprised to hear these bold words from timid Tuppeny. 'But how will you find out where she's gone?' asked Feefo.

'I shall climb the same tree as the Princess Lightheart and then I shall know what happened to her,' said Tuppeny, boldly.

'You dear, brave creature!' cried Lightfoot, and flung her arms round Tuppeny, who blushed with delight.

'I'd do anything in the world for such a dear, pretty little pixie,' he thought – but he didn't like to say it out loud.

'Come on, then,' said Jinks. 'Now or never!'

They set off down the garden path. Tiptoe, who was shaking a mat at her front door, saw them going and called out to know where. They told her.

'Goodness!' she said. 'I've heard of that bewitched tree before. Be careful, now, Tuppeny, or you'll disappear and never come back.'

They said goodbye to Tiptoe and went on their way to the woods. When they got there they hunted for the tree and soon found it because Lightfoot had carefully put a stick at the roots.

'That's it!' she said. 'Lightheart climbed right up to the top – and then vanished. Oh dear, oh dear, oh dear!'

'Oh, please don't cry!' said Tuppeny, in distress. 'I'll soon get your sister back again.'

He began to climb the tree. The others watched him. He climbed steadily up to the top, holding on tightly to the branches, calling out bravely to the others below.

And then, when he was almost at the top, he vanished! Yes, he really did! One minute he was there and the next he just wasn't!

'Tuppeny, Tuppeny!' shouted Jinks. But there was no answer.

'That's just what happened to Lightheart!' sobbed the little pixie princess. 'Oh, Tuppeny, now you've gone too!'

Jinks took out his handkerchief and wiped her eyes. Feefo gave another look upwards and then began to climb the tree as swiftly as he could.

'Feefo! Don't be silly!' cried Jinks. 'You'll vanish too!'

And sure enough, he did! Just at the top of the tree he disappeared into thin air. Not a sign of him was to be seen or heard!

Poor Jinks! He didn't know what in the world to do! There he was alone at the foot of the tree with the weeping little Princess.

'I'll climb up *nearly* to the top and see if I can find out anything,' he said at last to Lightfoot. 'Don't be afraid, now, I shan't go *right* to the top and vanish.'

So up he went, and stopped before he was quite to the top – and then, dear me, what a strange thing, he felt he must go on, and he climbed a few more steps.

Lightfoot, who was anxiously watching, suddenly gave a shriek. 'Don't go any higher, Jinks!'

But it was too late – Jinks too had gone! Then Lightfoot burst into sobs again and tore away through the wood, hurrying back to the kind-looking little fairy she had seen next door to the goblins' shop.

'Oh, oh!' she wept, when Tiptoe had run out to see what was the matter. 'They've *all* climbed the tree, and they've *all* disappeared.'

'Now what's all this?' suddenly cried a voice, and who should it be but the Nobbly Gnome come to see the three goblins. When Tiptoe told him what had happened he looked very solemn.

'A bad business,' he said, shaking his nobbly head. 'We must find out where they've gone.'

'But how can we when they are quite quite gone?' said Tiptoe, in despair.

'*I* shall go and find out!' said Nobbly.

'But you'll only disappear too,' said Lightfoot, dolefully.

'I daresay I shall,' said Nobbly. 'But *I* shall tie a long, long string to my foot, and when I disappear you must let the string unravel till it stops. Then you'll know I've got somewhere. I'll find some way of sending a message down the string to tell you where I've got to and how to rescue us.'

'How clever of you, Nobbly,' said Tiptoe, beaming all over her face. 'That really *is* a good idea. I don't know why the goblins say your brains are upside-down. I think you're very clever.'

Nobbly bought a most enormous ball of string. Then he and Tiptoe and the pixie Princess set off one more to the woods. When they came to the tree Nobbly said goodbye and climbed upwards, the string dangling down from his foot as he went. Tiptoe held the ball in her hand and it unravelled as Nobbly climbed.

Well, of course, the Nobbly Gnome vanished just as suddenly and completely as the others did. The string began to run out of the ball very quickly as soon as he disappeared and Tiptoe had hard work to hold it. At last, just as the string was nearly all gone, it stopped pulling out of the ball. Wherever Nobbly was he had stopped!

'Goodness knows how the gnome is going to send us a message down the string,' said Tiptoe, anxiously. 'We'd better sit down here and wait, even if it takes us all day.'

So they sat down and waited. The string hung quite still down the tree. Not even the wind moved it. Tiptoe leaned against the tree unhappily, thinking of all her missing friends. Poor little Lightfoot laid her head down on Tiptoe's knee and fell asleep. Soon Tiptoe closed her eyes and fell asleep too.

She was awakened by feeling the string jerking a little. She sat up and grasped her end firmly in her hand. It felt almost as if something or someone was coming down the string. Perhaps it was a message coming!

She woke Lightfoot and the two waited eagerly – and whatever *do* think came down the string? Guess!

Why, the little white mouse that always lived in Jinks's basket! What a surprise for Tiptoe! How pleased she was to see it!

'Ooh! A mouse!' said Lightfoot, with a squeal.

'Yes, it's Jinks's mouse!' said Tiptoe, and she picked up the little creature. It opened its mouth and a screwed-up piece of paper dropped out! A message, a message!

Tiptoe opened the paper and read the message:

'The top of this tree reaches into the Land of Nowhere. We are all here, quite safe, in an enormous castle, prisoners and servants of the Wise Witch, Konfundle-Rimminy. Please go and fetch the Red Whip from behind the mangle in the kitchen and tie the end of it to my mouse's tail. He is quite strong enough to drag it up the string. Give it to him tonight, then he will not be seen coming back. Don't worry about us. I will see that everyone comes back safely. Tell Lightfoot that Tuppeny sends his love and says that he will bring her sister back himself. JINKS.'

Tiptoe and Lightfoot wept for joy when they read the note. Tiptoe popped the mouse into her pocket, tied the end of the string safely to a branch and took Lightfoot back to the goblins' shop.

'It's no good going back to the tree until night,' said Tiptoe. 'So I think we'd better have something to eat. Oh, here is the Red Whip, behind the mangle, just as Jinks said. We'll take it into my cottage next door and then we'll have a good meal.'

They soon sat down and ate heartily, for they were very hungry. Then Tiptoe borrowed the goblins' car and she and Lightfoot set off to the palace where the little pixie's father and mother were waiting anxiously for their daughters' return.

They soon knew everything. Tiptoe asked them to send a hundred good soldiers to the tree in the wood, in case their help should be needed that night, and the King and Queen of Pixieland promised faithfully.

When it was dark Tiptoe and Lightfoot went to the woods, guarded well by a hundred good soldiers. When they got to the bewitched tree Tiptoe took out the little white mouse from her pocket. She carefully tied the thin end of the whip-lash to its tail, and then set it on the string that ran up into the darkness of the tree.

The little creature disappeared, dragging the Red Whip behind it. Soon both it and the Whip had disappeared.

The mouse, as soon as it had reached the top

of the tree, felt itself dragged by magic into the Land of Nowhere. It rose in a strong wind for some way and then fell to the ground. It heard the clatter of the Whip as that fell too. The mouse sniffed about for the string that would guide it to the Witch's castle. Soon it found it and, keeping it between its paws, ran swiftly along until it reached the dark, forbidding castle, with its small, slit-like windows lighted here and there.

The mouse went in at a small hole underneath the walls. The Whip dragged behind it and almost stuck. The mouse went back and nibbled the hole a little larger. It was a very intelligent creature, anxious to do its little best.

The Whip slipped through the hole. The mouse ran into a big hall and made for the stairway. Up the stairs it went, the Red Whip dragging behind it. Nobody was about, for it was in the middle of the night – but the mouse was half-afraid at any moment that the sharp-eared old witch would come popping out of a door. But nothing happened at all.

Up and up the mouse went, and up and up. At last it reached the very top of the castle. It came to a great yellow door, thick and solid. There was a small crack underneath and the mouse crept under it. The Whip followed. There was only just room for it.

Inside the room, which was perfectly round and very bare, sat the three goblins, Nobbly the gnome and a little pixie Princess, Lightheart, as pretty as Lightfoot, but a little bigger. She had been crying and Feefo had his arm round her, comforting her.

'Here's the mouse!' cried Jinks, holding up the candle as the mouse squeezed itself under the door! 'Oh, and it's brought the Whip! Good!'

The white mouse ran up to Jinks and he carefully untied the end of the whip-lash. He saw that the mouse's tail was red where the twine had rubbed it, so he took a little pot of ointment and smeared it on gently. The mouse squeaked gratefully and then ran up Jinks's leg and into the basket, where it sat down comfortably inside a roll of blue ribbon.

'Now!' said Jinks, looking round at the others. 'All we've got to do is to make a most enormous noise which will make the witch or her servants come to us, and then we will set the Whip on them – and if it acts like it did with the landlord of the Welcome Inn, my goodness, what a surprise our enemies will get! Be ready to escape as soon as there is a chance. Feefo, will you look after Princess Lightheart? Nobbly, you keep with Tuppeny. I will lead the way. Now then – everyone make as loud a noise as they can!'

At once a most fearful noise began! You should have heard it! Tuppeny roared at the top of his enormous voice. Lightheart squealed. Nobbly groaned in his deepest voice. Jinks shouted and yelled and stamped. And Feefo – well, Feefo did better than he had ever done before!

He thundered like three thunderstorms! He

roared like fifty dragons! He clanked like twelve engines gone wrong. He buzzed like a million bees! He jingled like a thousand bells! He was magnificent.

It was no wonder that the Witch Konfondle-Rimminy woke up from her sleep with a dreadful start and sat up in bed with all her hair standing on end. It was not surprising that her servants came howling in fright to her room, begging her to save them from whatever it was that was making such a terrible noise.

The witch listened. The noise was coming from the topmost room of the topmost tower. It was her prisoners! How dare they do that? How dare they wake her up! Aha, oho, grrrrrumph, wouldn't she just show them what she thought of people who did things like that!

Up she jumped and threw on her black cloak. She took her broomstick with her to beat her prisoners and, followed by all her servants, little black imps with bright green eyes, she flew up the long, long stairs on her broomstick.

'Sh! Here she comes!' said Jinks, who was listening at the door. 'Be quiet, now!'

Everyone was quiet. The witch fumbled for her key, put it into the lock and turned it. Then she unbolted the long bolts and threw open the door, glaring angrily.

'Whip, do your work!' shouted Jinks, and threw the Red Whip straight at the witch. And then – jumping beetles! How that Whip enjoyed itself! How it slashed and cracked! How it jumped here and darted there, getting in a cut at this little black imp and a slash at that one! The witch yelled when she felt it coiling round her and fled down the stairs, followed by all her imps in a fearful panic.

'Come on, quickly!' said Jinks to the others.

Feefo put his arm round Lightheart and helped her down the stairs. Tuppeny took Nobbly's hand and ran with him – and it was a good thing he did for Nobbly was in such a state of excitement that he might easily have run backwards or round and round, instead of down the stairs!

The Whip cleared the way beautifully for them. No matter where the witch hid or what she did, that Whip found her out and punished her for all the wicked deeds she had ever done! The black imps fled into cupboards and under chairs, but it wasn't a bit of good, the Whip poked them out!

Outside the castle it was dark, and Jinks stopped. 'Wait,' he said, feeling about. 'I must find that string that runs from Nobbly's foot to the bewitched tree. It's too dark to find the way ourselves.'

Tuppeny found it at last, and slowly they all followed Jinks, who let the string run through his hands as he went forward. Feefo had tight hold of Lightheart, who thought he was the nicest, kindest person she had ever met. Tuppeny had hold of Nobbly.

'Shall we be all right now, Jinks?' asked the little Princess, still half-frightened.

'Yes, I think so,' said Jinks. 'There's only

one thing that is worrying me. The witch will soon find out how to get rid of that Whip, for she is very clever – and what will happen when she comes after us? She has a whole army of black imps, you know.'

'Well, we must just hurry up, that's all,' said Feefo. 'Don't be frightened, Lightheart, *I'll* look after you.'

For some time there was no sound behind the little company hurrying along in the dark, guided by the string. Then Feefo's sharp ears heard something! It was the pattering of hundreds of tiny feet – the black imps!

'They're coming!' he cried to the others. 'Hurry!'

How they hurried – but the pattering behind grew louder and louder, and Jinks felt sure the witch was coming too, riding on her big broomstick!

Suddenly Jinks's foot knocked against something and the string seemed to disappear downwards.

'Here's the tree!' he cried, thankfully. 'If only we can get down it quickly!'

Down they all climbed in the dark, Feefo half-carrying little Lightheart – and climbing behind them, squealing and squawking, came

hundreds of black imps, with the witch behind them!

But what a surprise! At the bottom of the tree was the big army of soldiers sent by the King and Queen of Pixieland! They drew their swords, which glinted in the light of many lanterns, and the black imps, terrified, swarmed back up the tree, crying 'We're afraid, we're afraid!'

'We'll cut down the tree before the old witch climbs down herself!' cried Jinks.

But no one had an axe! So Jinks quickly

opened his basket, and there, right in the front, was a sharp axe! Good!

He took it and at once began to chop the bewitched tree. The axe was sharp and Jinks was strong.

'Move away!' cried the goblin. 'The tree will fall!'

Everyone moved to a safe distance and watched. Suddenly Nobbly gave a shout and pointed up the tree.

'The witch is climbing down!'

So she was – but Jinks didn't stop his work. Chop – chop – chop – the axe bit deep into the tree and, just as the old witch Konfondle-Rimminy was half-way down the tree, down it came with a groan and a crash!

The witch fell too – and as she touched the ground she disappeared into smoke!

'That's the end of *her*!' cried Jinks. 'Now we're all right! Hurrah!'

'Look! The dawn is coming!' cried Nobbly, pointing to the east. Everyone stood and watched the sun rise, a big golden ball that lighted up the wood and made everything new and beautiful.

'We must take the Princesses back to their parents,' said the Captain of the soldiers. 'I expect the King and Queen of Pixieland will send for you to thank you and reward you for your great help some time during the day.'

'Goodbye, darling Feefo,' said Princess Lightheart, hugging Feefo.

'Goodbye, darling Tuppeny,' said Princess Lightfoot, and she hugged fat little Tuppeny, who was simply delighted.

The soldiers marched away with the Princesses, and the goblins, Nobbly and Fairy Tiptoe went back to Hollyhock Cottage, talking nineteen to the dozen all the way.

'It *was* good and brave and clever of you to come and rescue us like that,' said Jinks to Nobbly. 'I don't know what we'd have done without you and dear Tiptoe. We should never have escaped from that tower in the Land of Nowhere!'

'We'd better all have a little sleep before we do anything,' said Tiptoe, yawning. 'If you've got to go to the Court of the King of Pixieland, goblins, you'll have to look your smartest, too, you know. I expect you'll get a fine reward.'

'Well, you and Nobbly shall share it all!' said Jinks. 'You are the best friends anyone could have!'

Soon all of them were fast asleep. They were awakened by loud knocking on the door – messengers from the King of Pixieland begging the three goblins, the gnome and the Fairy Tiptoe to attend at the Court at three o'clock that afternoon.

'Jumping beetles!' said Tuppeny, excited. 'What adventurous lives we lead nowadays! Where's my best suit?'

They spent the rest of the morning getting ready. How grand they all were, to be sure! In brand-new green and yellow suits, with yellow feathers in their jaunty green hats, the goblins were a sight to see. Nobbly had really washed himself well for once, and wore a red tunic with green stockings, and a funny round cap with little feathers sticking up all round the rim.

Tiptoe looked the loveliest of them all. She had on a new frock made of cornflowers and she wore a blue fillet round her lovely hair. Jinks looked and looked at her. She was prettier than a princess, really!

They all packed themselves into the little green car and drove off to the palace. Six heralds with long golden trumpets were awaiting them and sounded a fine fanfare as the car drew up at the gates. Footmen dressed in blue and silver took them into the palace, which, although it was not nearly so grand as the King of Fairyland's palace, was really very beautiful.

The King and Queen were sitting on their thrones, wearing their crowns. Beside them, one on each side, sat the Princesses Lightfoot and Lightheart, looking very lovely in their crowns and long red cloaks.

The three goblins and the gnome went up and bowed low to Their Majesties. Tiptoe was shy and hung back, but Princess Lightfoot jumped up and drew her down beside her.

'We are very grateful to you all for rescuing our Princess Lightheart from the Land of Nowhere,' said the King. 'We wish to thank you and reward you. Ask what you please and you shall have it. What do you wish? A palace? Gold? Precious stones?'

'I don't really think there's anything I want, thank you, Your Majesty,' said Jinks. 'I am very happy as I am.'

'Well,' said Tuppeny, blushing a bright red, 'there's only one thing *I* want, Your Majesty.'

'What is that?' asked the King, kindly.

'Well – you see – it's like this – ' stammered Tuppeny. 'I'd like – very much like – to marry that dear little Princess Lightfoot – if she'd have me, that is.'

'Oooooh!' squealed Lightfoot in delight and she rushed at Tuppeny and hugged him. 'Oh, Father, may I? He's so kind and brave and jolly.'

'And *I'd* like to marry Lightheart!' said Feefo, boldly. 'That's the only reward *I* want.'

'But, bless us all, you haven't even got a palace, or a present to offer my daughters!' cried the King.

'Oh, yes, we've a fine palace,' said Feefo, at once. 'The King of Fairyland gave it to us for something we did for him. And as for a present – here is a pearl necklace made of the famous pearls our black cat drops from its mouth when it purrs!'

At the same moment Tuppeny took a pearl

necklace from his pocket, and Feefo took one from his and they both knelt down in front of the Princesses and offered the lovely, gleaming beads to them.

'Well, if Lightfoot and Lightheart wish to marry you, then that shall be your reward,' said the King at last. 'You seem to be brave and good little goblins. Come back tomorrow and we will have the wedding. Then you can all go off to your palace and live happily ever afterwards!'

'Oh, thank you, Your Majesty!' said Feefo and Tuppeny, delighted. They bowed, kissed the Princesses goodbye and went backwards out of the King's presence, red with excitement and delight. Nobbly, Feefo and Tiptoe followed.

Jinks said nothing at all as they drove home. He looked very miserable.

'What's the matter?' asked Tuppeny, when they were all having a good tea at Hollyhock Cottage.

'Matter enough,' said Jinks. 'What am I going to do without you two? Will Nobbly come to live with me?'

'Oh no,' said Nobbly, at once. 'I love living in a palace and it will be such fun having the

100

two Princesses and Tuppeny and Feefo there too.'

'I shall be very lonely,' said Jinks, sadly. Then he felt a little hand slipped into his and saw Tiptoe's sweet face smiling at him.

'Why need you be lonely?' she said. 'Don't you like me? Couldn't *we* get married too and go and live at the palace as well?'

'Oh Tiptoe, of course!' cried everyone in delight. 'Why ever didn't we think of it before! Of course you must marry Jinks and come and live at the palace too! What fun! And we'll keep this little cottage for ourselves, so that sometimes we can come back here and remember the fine times we have had together.'

'What about Nobbly?' asked Jinks. 'There's no one for *him* to marry.'

'*That* doesn't matter,' said Tuppeny. 'What good would a wife be to Nobbly? He'd forget all about her, and shut her up in the dog-kennel or something.'

'Yes, I should,' said Nobbly, sighing. 'I shall be quite happy just living with you all. It will be so nice to have meals all together!'

Well, the next day they were all married, and the wedding was the grandest one held for a hundred years. Bells rang, trumpets sounded,

people cheered, and everything was as merry as could be.

Then the three goblins took their pretty little wives and rode with them in a grand coach to their palace, Nobbly followed behind driving the little green car. All the people cheered as they passed.

'Hail to Prince Jinks and his wife Fairy Tiptoe! Hail to Prince Feefo and the Princess Lightheart! Hail to Prince Tuppeny and the Princess Lightfoot!'

'Jumping beetles!' said Tuppeny, happily. 'Listen to that! We're princes now!'

'You deserve it!' shouted Nobbly, behind them. 'Three cheers for us all!'

And now they are all *very* busy indeed, trying to live happily ever after.

Join the RED FOX Reader's Club

The Red Fox Readers' Club is for readers of all ages. All you have to do is ask your local bookseller or librarian for a Red Fox Reader's Club card. As an official Red Fox Reader you will qualify for your own Red Fox Reader's Clubpack – full of exciting surprises! If you have any difficulty obtaining a Red Fox Readers' Club card please write to: Random House Children's Books Marketing Department, 20 Vauxhall Bridge Road, London SW1V 2SA.

Other great reads ✒ *from* **Red Fox**

Further Red Fox titles that you might enjoy reading are listed on the following pages. They are available in bookshops or they can be ordered directly from us.

If you would like to order books, please send this form and the money due to:

ARROW BOOKS, BOOKSERVICE BY POST, PO BOX 29, DOUGLAS, ISLE OF MAN, BRITISH ISLES. Please enclose a cheque or postal order made out to Arrow Books Ltd for the amount due, plus 75p per book for postage and packing to a maximum of £7.50, both for orders within the UK. For customers outside the UK, please allow £1.00 per book.

NAME_____

ADDRESS_____

_____

Please print clearly.

Whilst every effort is made to keep prices low, it is sometimes necessary to increase cover prices at short notice. If you are ordering books by post, to save delay it is advisable to phone to confirm the correct price. The number to ring is THE SALES DEPARTMENT 071 (if outside London) 973 9700.

Other great reads *from **Red Fox***

Animal stories from Enid Blyton

If you like reading stories about animals, you'll love Enid Blyton's animal books.

THE BIRTHDAY KITTEN

Terry and Tessie want a pet for their birthday – but when the big day comes, they're disappointed.

ISBN 0 09 924100 5   £1.99

THE BIRTHDAY KITTEN and THE BOY WHO WANTED A DOG

A great value two-books-in-one containing two stories about children and their lovable pets.

ISBN 0 09 977930 7   £2.50

HEDGEROW TALES

Go on a journey through the woodlands and fields and meet the fascinating animals who live there.

ISBN 0 09 980880 3   £2.50

MORE HEDGEROW TALES

A second set of animal stories packed with accurate details.

ISBN 0 09 980880 3   £2.50

THE ADVENTURES OF SCAMP

Scamp the puppy is nothing but a bundle of mischief – and he does get into a lot of trouble.

ISBN 0 09 987860 7   £2.99

Other great reads from **Red Fox**

All the fun of the fair with Enid Blyton's circus stories

Roll up! Roll up! Discover Enid Blyton's exciting circus stories for yourself. They're full of adventure and thrills, with a colourful cast of funny and unusual characters and lovable animals. Join the children who live in the circus and enjoy all the fun of the fair for yourself.

MR GALLIANO'S CIRCUS

Jimmy loves the circus – how can he bear it to leave town? Is there *any* hope he might go with it?

ISBN 0 09 954170 X   £1.75

CIRCUS DAYS AGAIN

A new ringleader arrives at Mr Galliano's circus – and, oh dear! No one can *bear* him . . .

ISBN 0 09 954180 7   £1.75

COME TO THE CIRCUS

Fenella is terrified of animals. Imagine her horror when she discovers she is going to live in Mr Carl Crack's circus!

ISBN 0 09 937590 7   £1.75

THREE BOYS AND A CIRCUS

Orphan Dick is thrilled to find a job at the circus – but he has an enemy who wants him to leave.

ISBN 0 09 987870 4   £2.99

Other great reads from **Red Fox**

Magical books from Enid Blyton

Enter the world of fairyland with the magical stories of Enid Blyton – and enjoy tales of goblins, pixies, fairies and all sorts of strange and wonderful things.

UP THE FARAWAY TREE

If you climb to the top of the Faraway Tree, you can reach all sorts of wonderful places . . .

ISBN 0 09 942720 6 £2.50

THE GOBLIN AEROPLANE AND OTHER STORIES

Jill and Robert are working outside when they are whisked away on a strange adventure . . .

ISBN 0 09 973590 3 £2.50

HOLIDAY STORIES

A lovely collection of stories with some magical characters.

ISBN 0 09 987850 X £1.99

THE LITTLE GREEN IMP AND OTHER STORIES

An enchanting collection of stories about some very special people – including the mischievous green imp.

ISBN 0 09 938940 1 £1.50

RUN-ABOUT'S HOLIDAY

Run-About is Robin and Betty's magical friend – and life is never dull when he's around!

ISBN 0 09 926040 9 £1.50

Other great reads ✤ *from* **Red Fox**

Magical books from Enid Blyton

Enter the world of fairyland with the magical stories of Enid Blyton – and enjoy tales of goblins, pixies, fairies and all sorts of strange and wonderful things.

UP THE FARAWAY TREE

If you climb to the top of the Faraway Tree, you can reach all sorts of wonderful places . . .

ISBN 0 09 942720 6   £2.50

THE GOBLIN AEROPLANE AND OTHER STORIES

Jill and Robert are working outside when they are whisked away on a strange adventure . . .

ISBN 0 09 973590 3   £2.50

HOLIDAY STORIES

A lovely collection of stories with some magical characters.

ISBN 0 09 987850 X   £1.99

THE LITTLE GREEN IMP AND OTHER STORIES

An enchanting collection of stories about some very special people – including the mischievous green imp.

ISBN 0 09 938940 1   £1.50

RUN-ABOUT'S HOLIDAY

Run-About is Robin and Betty's magical friend – and life is never dull when he's around!

ISBN 0 09 926040 9   £1.50

THE FIRST GREEN GOBLIN STORYBOOK

When three goblins team up offering to help *anyone* do *anything* life becomes full of adventures for them . . .

ISBN 0 09 993700 X   £2.99

THE ENID BLYTON NEWSLETTER

Would you like to receive The Enid Blyton Newsletter? It has lots of news about Enid Blyton books, videos, plays, etc. There are also puzzles and a page for your letters. It is published three times a year and is free for children who live in the United Kingdom and Ireland.

If you would like to receive it for a year, please write to: The Enid Blyton Newsletter, PO Box No. 357, London WC2E 9HQ, sending your name and address. (UK and Ireland only).